27.12

DATE DUE	
DEC 4 - 2001	MAY 2 5 2004
JAN 1 3 2002	JUL 2 2005
MAY 2 5 2002	
SEP 2 8 2002	MAR 1 8 2006
	MAR 2 1 2007
DEC 1 8 2002	AUG 1 4 2007
APR 2 5 2003	
JUN 2 0 2003	
DEC 1 3 2003	
FEB 2 2 2004	

DEMCO, INC. 38-2931

FEB 16 1999

The Deep Blue Planet

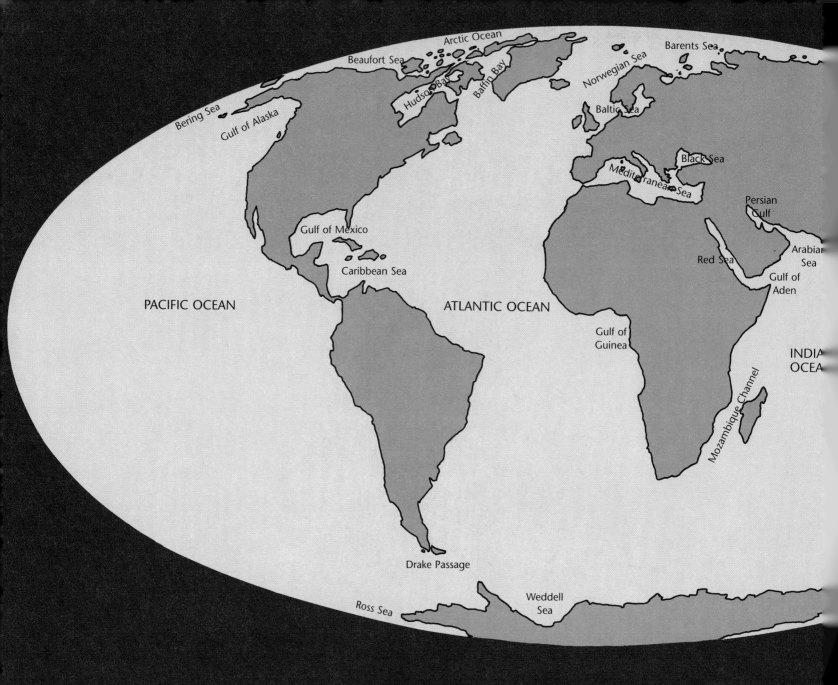

Arctic Ocean

Beaufort Sea

Baffin Bay

Hudson Bay

Barents Sea

Norwegian Sea

Bering Sea

Gulf of Alaska

Baltic Sea

Black Sea

Mediterranean Sea

Persian Gulf

PACIFIC OCEAN

Gulf of Mexico

Caribbean Sea

ATLANTIC OCEAN

Red Sea

Arabian Sea

Gulf of Aden

Gulf of Guinea

INDIAN OCEAN

Mozambique Channel

Drake Passage

Ross Sea

Weddell Sea

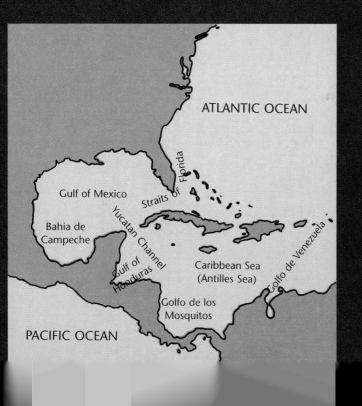

ATLANTIC OCEAN

Florida

Straits of

Gulf of Mexico

Yucatan Channel

Bahia de Campeche

Caribbean Sea (Antilles Sea)

Golfo de Venezuela

Gulf of Honduras

Golfo de los Mosquitos

PACIFIC OCEAN

Norwegian Sea

Barents Sea

ATLANTIC OCEAN

White Sea

North Sea

Baltic Sea

Bay of Biscay

Tyrrhenian Sea

Adriatic Sea

Caspian Sea

Black Sea

Mediterranean Sea

Ionian Sea

Aegean Sea

Gulf of Sidra

Red Sea

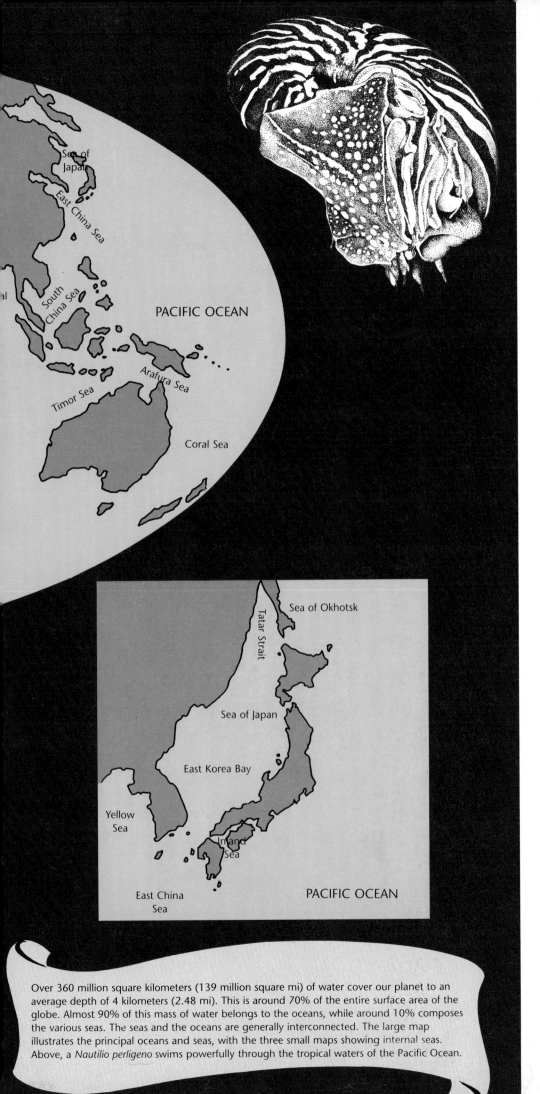

OCEANS AND SEAS

Sea of Japan

East China Sea

South China Sea

PACIFIC OCEAN

Arafura Sea

Timor Sea

Coral Sea

Sea of Okhotsk

Tatar Strait

Sea of Japan

East Korea Bay

Yellow Sea

Inland Sea

East China Sea

PACIFIC OCEAN

Over 360 million square kilometers (139 million square mi) of water cover our planet to an average depth of 4 kilometers (2.48 mi). This is around 70% of the entire surface area of the globe. Almost 90% of this mass of water belongs to the oceans, while around 10% composes the various seas. The seas and the oceans are generally interconnected. The large map illustrates the principal oceans and seas, with the three small maps showing internal seas. Above, a *Nautilio perligeno* swims powerfully through the tropical waters of the Pacific Ocean.

The Deep Blue Planet

OCEANS AND SEAS

ALEX VOGLINO AND RENATO MASSA
ENGLISH TRANSLATION BY NEIL FRAZER DAVENPORT

RSVP
**RAINTREE
STECK-VAUGHN**
PUBLISHERS
The Steck-Vaughn Company

Austin, Texas

Published by Raintree Steck-Vaughn Publishers, an imprint of Steck-Vaughn Company

Editors
Caterina Longanesi, Linda Zierdt-Warshaw, William P. Mara

Design and layout
Jaca Book Design Office

Library of Congress Cataloging-in-Publication Data

Voglino, Alex.
    [Mare oceano. English]
    Oceans and seas / Alex Voglino and Renato Massa ; English translation by Neil Frazer Davenport.
       p.   cm. — (The deep blue planet)
    Includes bibliographical references and index.
    Summary: Presents an in-depth analysis of the ocean environment, including sediments, waves, currents, tides, salinity, and the properties of seawater.
    ISBN 0-8172-4650-9
    1. Ocean — Juvenile literature. [1. Ocean.] I. Massa, Renato. II. Title. III. Series.
GC21.5.V6413   1998
551.46 — dc21   96–40487
                                         CIP   AC

Printed and bound in the United States
1 2 3 4 5 6 7 8 9 0 WO 01 00 99 98 97

CONTENTS

Please note: words in **bold** can also be found in the glossary. They are bold only the first time they appear in the main body of the text.

INTRODUCTION

The oceans and seas are wondrous places of both dark and light, flora and fauna, warm and cold, and life and death. Many regions are still largely unknown to us, so there is little doubt that hundreds of mysteries still lie in their murky depths.

The oceans and seas cover just over 70 percent of the Earth. They have provided us with many pieces to the puzzle of how life began on this planet, since the earliest forms of life were thought to have existed there. The rocks and sediment along the ocean floor have yielded a great deal of fossil evidence over the years.

The value of the oceans and seas is immeasurable. They have given us many useful chemicals and minerals, including bromine, magnesium, and salt, not to mention pearls for jewelry and shells for building material and health supplements. Most experts believe we have not yet realized their full potential in regard to nutrition, though it is believed that humans derive at least 10% of their overall protein from the Earth's waters, either directly or indirectly. Finally, there is the recreational aspect. Activities such as swimming, fishing, boating, diving, and so on, when executed properly and responsibly, provide us with a great deal of pleasure and a measure of relief from the grind of our daily lives.

Sadly, however, we humans have caused some serious damage to the oceans and seas in recent times. Industry is the greatest violator, with over a quarter of a million manufacturing facilities using the great bodies of water as dumping grounds for their often highly dangerous waste products, including mercury, lead, sulfuric acid, and asbestos. In addition, towns and cities regularly dump improperly treated sewage and millions of tons of paper and plastic wastes into rivers, streams, and lakes. Plastics in particular have the potential to remain intact for hundreds of years.

However, we have not yet reached a point of no return, and one of the goals of the *Deep Blue Planet* books is to give you a deeper understanding of—and in turn a deeper appreciation and respect for—the aquatic environments of this world. The more you know about any subject, the greater your appreciation for it will be, and the oceans and seas are in desperate need of increased appreciation. Perhaps someday you will make efforts of your own to preserve these beautiful natural areas and the myriad life forms that thrive within them. If so, you will be helping to guarantee them the bright and vibrant future they so richly deserve.

THE OCEAN FLOOR

The Continental Margin

The first topographical charts of the ocean floor were drawn during the two-year research expedition to the South Atlantic by the German ship *Meteor* between 1925 and 1927. The mapmakers used a new instrument called an echo-sounder, or sonar. Since then we have gained an increasingly detailed knowledge of the ocean floor. This technology allows us to measure its depth and form through the analysis of sound **waves** bounced off the bottom.

Today it is well known that the profile of the sea floor is highly varied and that many of its characteristics are repeated.

However, before talking about the **deep-sea floor** we must begin with coastal regions. It is from here that the **continental margin** projects outwards toward the open sea. The continental margin can be divided into three main sections: the **continental shelf**, the **continental slope**, and the **continental rise**.

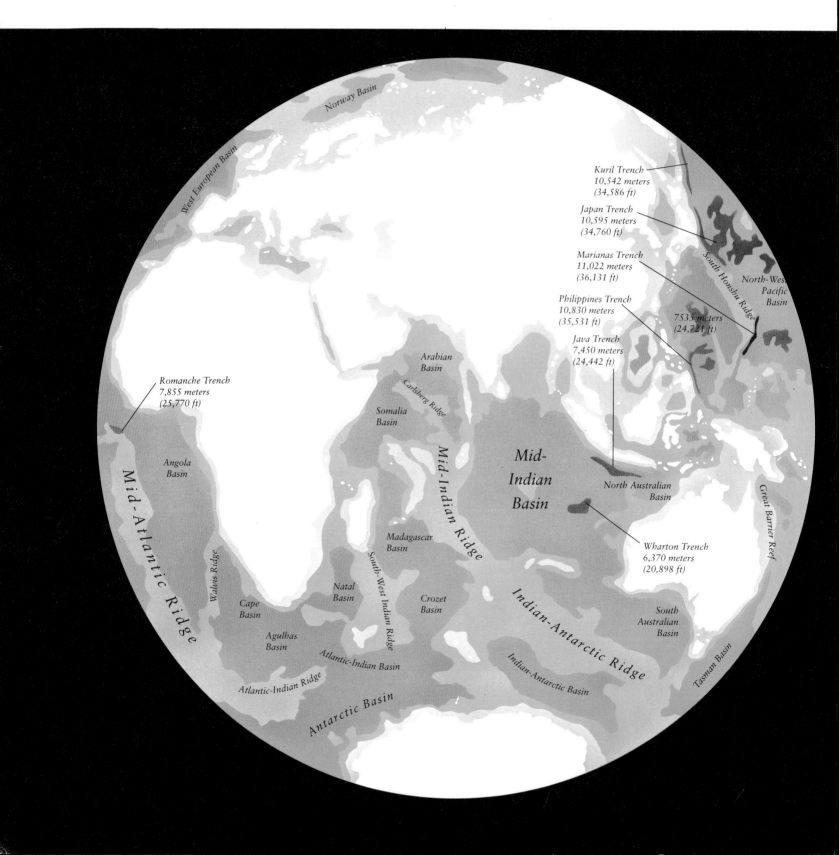

The bottom of the sea is anything but uniform: it features plains, mountains, trenches, and escarpments, and is divided into a variety of zones, with particular morphological characteristics according to their depths. The profile of the seas and oceans is very varied. Nevertheless, it is possible (provided you have suitable research equipment) to recognize a number of fundamental morphological features of the ocean floors—just like the mountains, rivers, and lakes of dry land—that tend to be repeated throughout the globe.

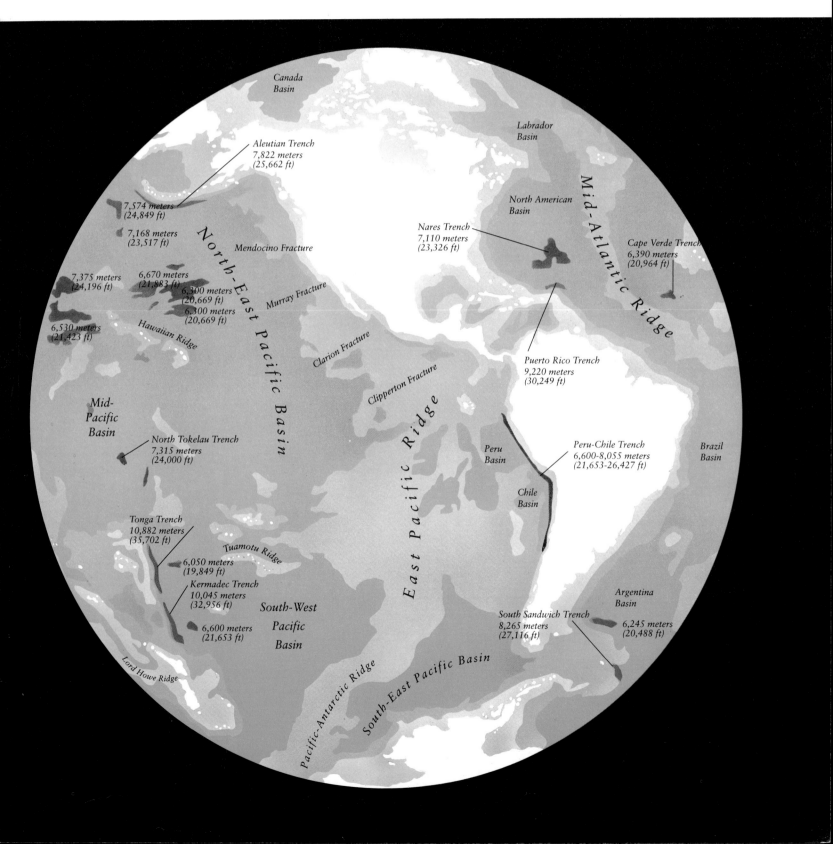

Canada Basin

Labrador Basin

Aleutian Trench
7,822 meters
(25,662 ft)

North American Basin

Mid-Atlantic Ridge

7,574 meters
(24,849 ft)

Nares Trench
7,110 meters
(23,326 ft)

Cape Verde Trench
6,390 meters
(20,964 ft)

7,168 meters
(23,517 ft)

North-East Pacific Basin

Mendocino Fracture

7,375 meters
(24,196 ft)

6,670 meters
(21,883 ft)

6,300 meters
(20,669 ft)

6,300 meters
(20,669 ft)

Murray Fracture

6,530 meters
(21,423 ft)

Hawaiian Ridge

Clarion Fracture

Puerto Rico Trench
9,220 meters
(30,249 ft)

Clipperton Fracture

Mid-Pacific Basin

East Pacific Ridge

North Tokelau Trench
7,315 meters
(24,000 ft)

Peru Basin

Peru-Chile Trench
6,600-8,055 meters
(21,653-26,427 ft)

Brazil Basin

Chile Basin

Tonga Trench
10,882 meters
(35,702 ft)

Tuamotu Ridge

6,050 meters
(19,849 ft)

Kermadec Trench
10,045 meters
(32,956 ft)

South-West Pacific Basin

Argentina Basin

South Sandwich Trench
8,265 meters
(27,116 ft)

6,245 meters
(20,488 ft)

6,600 meters
(21,653 ft)

Lord Howe Ridge

Pacific-Antarctic Ridge

South-East Pacific Basin

The continental shelf extends below the surface of the sea from the shore, sloping gently until it reaches a depth of between 100 and 200 meters (328 to 656 ft). Occasionally the continental shelf may extend hundreds of kilometers from the coast, as it does in the North Sea or the Adriatic Sea. Usually it extends only a short distance, and of all the Earth's surface that is found underwater, only 8% of it belongs to the continental shelf. Since the relatively shallow water covering the continental shelf allows sunlight to penetrate fully, the shelf is the region with the greatest **density** of animal and plant life in the marine environment.

At a certain point, the continental shelf plunges steeply downward. This section is the continental slope. In some areas, especially along the margins of the Atlantic Ocean, the continental slope becomes less steep and forms the continental rise.

Frequently, and especially around the mouths of large rivers, the continental slope is slashed by deep underwater valleys. These valleys are the result of two processes. First of all, during the ice ages, the level of the oceans was lower than it is now, and the continental slope was part of the dry land rather than underwater. Rivers ran across the slope and eroded its surface, digging deep gorges which became underwater valleys when the sea level rose again. The effects of this first process were then amplified by underwater rockslides. As the sediments created by the rockslides slipped down the continental slope, they further eroded the surface, making the existing valleys deeper while creating new ones at the same time.

The Geography of the Depths

The deep-sea floor that extends beyond the continental rise is younger than the ocean itself because it is constantly renewed. An immense range of mountains lies at the bottom of all the oceans. This continuous range makes up the **mid-ocean ridges**. It is formed exclusively from basaltic rocks. In some sections the rock is split by great vertical fractures, but generally the ridges run unbroken through the oceans for over 40,000 kilometers (24,855 mi). Along the crests of almost the entire length of the ridges are endless furrows. The two sides of the furrows tend to spread away from each other because **magma** from the Earth's **mantle** continuously rises through them. When this magma solidifies, it forms new ocean floor. As it solidifies, the rock is magnetized according to the direction of the Earth's **magnetic field**. As a consequence of the continual expansion of the ridge toward the two sides of the furrow, a band or stripe of rock is created with a very precise magnetic "signature."

Most of the ocean floor is composed of vast plains with inclines of less than 1:1000. These regions are called **abyssal plains**. The plains are found both close to the continental land masses (as in the western Mediterranean) and in open sea (off Australia, New Zealand, North America, etc.).

The bottom of the sea also features **deep-sea trenches**, volcanoes, and submarine mountains, the formation of which depends on the dynamics of the ocean floor and is explained in the next chapter.

Section through the major geological formations of the ocean basins.

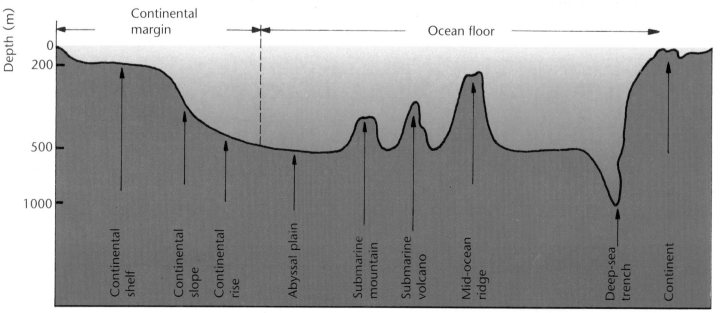

Continental shelf	Continental slope	Continental rise	Abyssal plain	Submarine mountain	Submarine volcano	Mid-ocean ridge	Deep-sea trench	Continent	

Depth (m)

Continental margin — Ocean floor

0
200
500
1000

THE DYNAMICS OF THE OCEAN FLOOR

Plate Tectonics

The theory of continental drift was mentioned in print as long ago as 1912, by the German geographer Alfred Wegener. The theory has now been further developed and is known as plate **tectonics**. It is based on the idea that the Earth's **crust** is not a single continuous surface, but instead is divided into adjacent segments. These segments are composed of eight **continental plates** plus a number of smaller plates, with a maximum thickness of around 100 kilometers (62 mi). The plates float like rafts on the **asthenosphere**. The asthenosphere is the semi-liquid upper layer of the underlying mantle; that is to say the intermediate and the inner layers of the Earth. The movement of the plates making up the Earth's surface also causes the continents (those parts of the plates above sea level) to move. The continents move with respect to each other, edge against edge, colliding and riding up over one another.

When two plates move away from each other, a gap is created. Molten rock or magma from the mantle below rises to fill this gap. When the magma solidifies, it creates the new borders of the plates. At the same time, the opposite edge of the plate is pushing against its neighbor. The

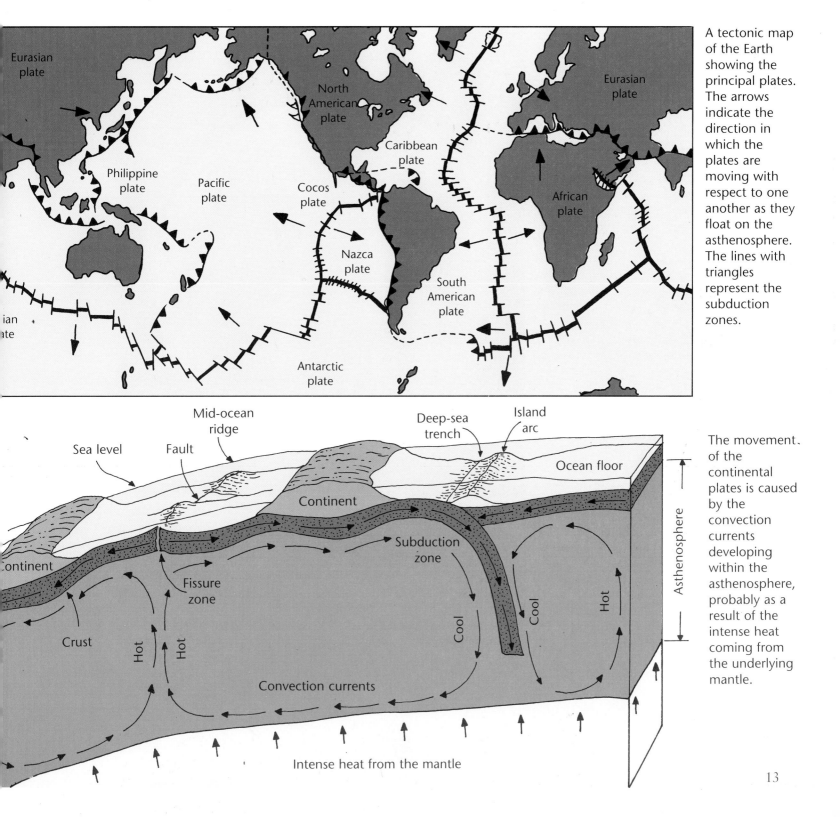

A tectonic map of the Earth showing the principal plates. The arrows indicate the direction in which the plates are moving with respect to one another as they float on the asthenosphere. The lines with triangles represent the subduction zones.

The movement of the continental plates is caused by the convection currents developing within the asthenosphere, probably as a result of the intense heat coming from the underlying mantle.

edge of the advancing plate may dip below the other plate and sink into the asthenosphere up to 100 kilometers (62 mi) or more below the surface. This process is called **subduction**. **Deep-sea trenches** are formed in the so-called subduction zone and may reach depths as great as 11,000 meters (36,089 ft), as in the case of the Mariana Trench in the West Pacific. Alternatively, the two neighboring plates may crush into each other and rise up to create great mountain ranges, like the Himalayas and the Alps.

Oceanic Magma Islands

The plates do not have a constant thickness, nor do they move at a constant speed. For its part, the magma below the plates may be more or less fluid. The formation of the enormous submarine volcanoes depends on the combination of these factors. When a relatively thin plate slides over a point at which the magma is particularly fluid, the magma may "perforate" the plate and burst onto the ocean floor, creating a volcano. When the volcano emerges above sea level, an **oceanic island** is created. In the tropical regions, a coral atoll may form around the island.

The so-called **hot spots** are a particular form of the process just described. The best-known example is probably the Hawaiian archipelago. The islands that make up the archipelago are arranged in a line running from the southeast to the northwest. The southeastern extremity is represented by the island of Hawaii itself, which is practically a single, enormous, active volcano. The islands are arranged in a line because of the hot spot—imagine a cauldron of boiling **lava** that is fixed in one place while a plate (in this case the oceanic crust of the Pacific) moves slowly above it. When the lava finds a weak point, it begins to burn through the crust like a blowtorch and ultimately erupts onto the ocean floor, giving rise to a volcanic island. The plate, however, continues to move over the "cauldron," cutting off the flow of magma until the next weak point arrives and another volcanic island is formed. If the plate moves in a constant direction, a line of volcanic islands will be created.

Young Ocean Floors

The fact that the old ocean floor is destroyed while the new floor is being created provides the answer to a puzzling aspect of marine geology. The oceans have almost always existed on the Earth, and yet none of the sediments found on their floors are more then 150 million years old. The average is just 80 million years old. This means the ocean floors are younger than the waters above them, since the oldest sediments, together with the crust that supported them, have sunk into the asthenosphere or have become part of one of the mountain ranges along the plate edges.

If we know how fast, and in which direction, the plates are moving, we can formulate hypotheses about how the continents and oceans have changed in the past and how they will continue to change in the future. For example, on the basis of this theory, scientists have been able to deduce that the area occupied by the Atlantic Ocean has grown over the last 150 million years, while the area occupied

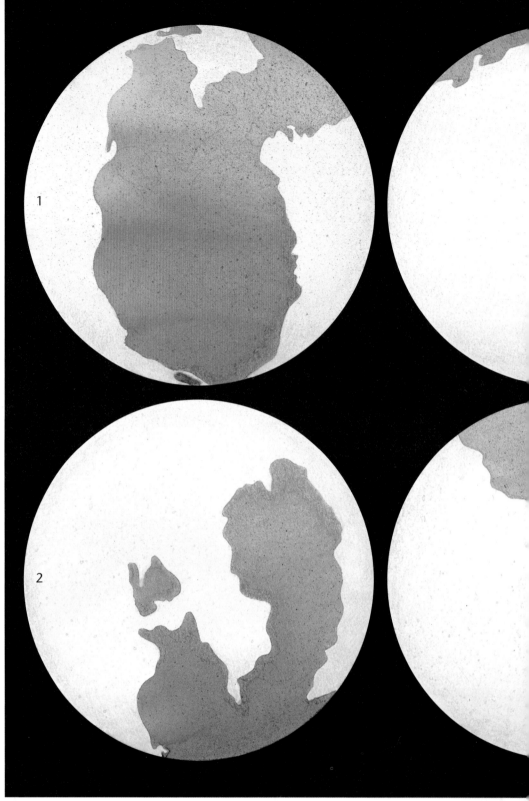

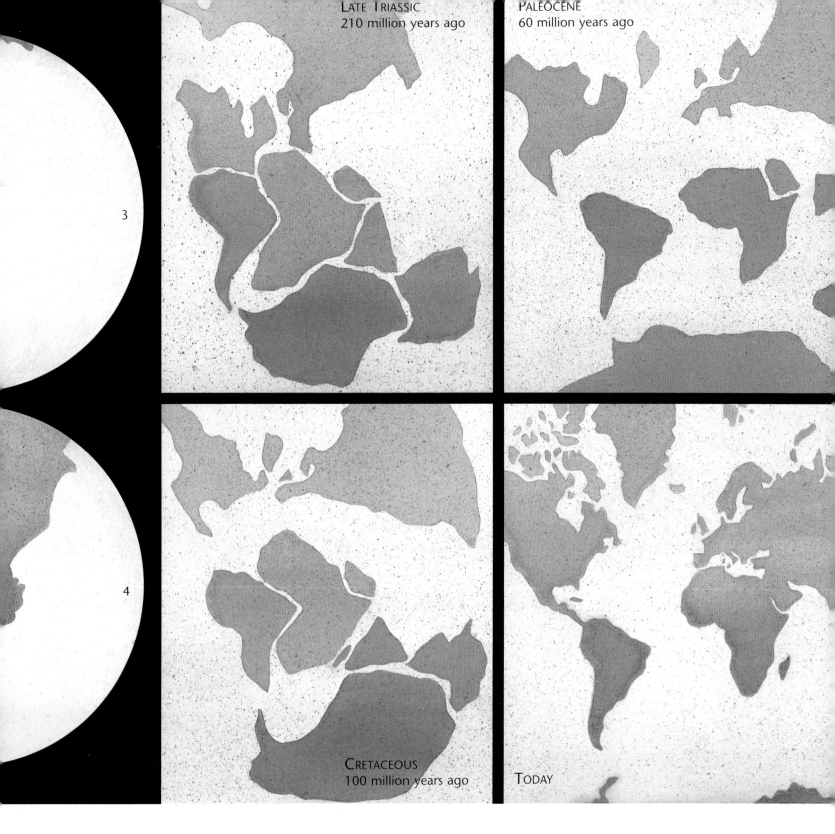

LATE TRIASSIC
210 million years ago

PALEOCENE
60 million years ago

CRETACEOUS
100 million years ago

TODAY

3

4

by the Pacific has shrunk.

There is convincing evidence that all the land masses were united in one supercontinent, known as **Pangaea**, up until about 200 million years ago. This supercontinent began to break up due to plate movements in the Mesozoic Era, about 180 million years ago. This process eventually led to the creation of the continents as we know them today.

Left: According to the theory of continental drift, up until 200 million years ago all the continental land masses were united in a single supercontinent, named Pangaea in 1912 by Alfred Wegener, the author of the theory. The diagrams here show four views of Pangaea, from four different cardinal points, during the Permian Period (290-250 million years ago).

Above: Around 180 million years ago, in the Mesozoic Era, the movement of the tectonic plates led to the breakup of Pangaea and, over time, to the formation of the continents as we know them today. The proof of this process comes on the one hand from an examination of the orientation of the paleomagnetism of the rocks, and on the other through the distribution of the large reptiles of the past. When the fossilized remains of the same species of dinosaur are found in such diverse places as Africa, South America and Antarctica, it is reasonable to suppose that at one time these regions were connected.

THE EXPANDING EARTH

Paleomagnetism

The most convincing evidence supporting the theory of plate tectonics and the expansion of the ocean floors comes from studies of the variations in the Earth's magnetic field through the geological ages. In their fluid state, the magnetic materials tend to align themselves according to the direction of the magnetic field in which they find themselves. When the rock cools, this alignment is "frozen" and represents a record of the alignment of the Earth's magnetic field at that particular moment. Since the variations in the Earth's magnetic field have been dated, the magnetism of the rocks allows us to date the rocks themselves.

In the early 1960s, studies of the **paleomagnetism** of rock in South America and Africa had already demonstrated the validity of Wegener's original hypothesis. Wegener had based his ideas almost exclusively on visual evidence. He drew attention to the fact that the profiles of the African and South American continents corresponded, as did those of the northwestern coast of Africa and the eastern coast of North America. Paleomagnetism has allowed us to discover that the rocks in the coastal regions of South America and Africa also correspond in terms of their magnetic alignment. It is therefore reasonably possible that the two continents were joined together during the mid to late Triassic Period (around 200 million years ago).

The study of paleomagnetism has also allowed us to clearly demonstrate the process of the expansion of the ocean floors. It has been proven that the ocean crust presents a series of magnetic alignments in bands parallel to the mid-ocean ridge. The relative magnetic fields are in turn aligned to the north or to the south. The magnetic fields alternate symmetrically on both sides of the ridge. This appears to demonstrate that new ocean crust is continually generated from the ocean ridge, and that the crust on either side of the ridge moves away in opposite directions as new magma solidifies.

The Earth's Crust Through Geologic Time

Geophysicists have used this theory to reconstruct the stages of growth of the ocean basins. All of the theoretical models in this fascinating story were at first based on the assumptions that 1) the Earth has always been the same size and 2) that its radius has remained unchanged throughout geological time. If this were true, however, the total production of new ocean crust would have had to be balanced, during those hundreds of millions of years, by the destruction of an equal quantity of old crust, occurring when the crust sinks into the asthenosphere.

However, there is evidence of a degree of irregularity in the rate of the production of new crust compared with the destruction of old crust. The data that is available today actually suggests that the Earth's crust is constantly expanding. In practice this means that more material leaves the mantle than is returned to it through the subduction of plate margins. There even is a hypothesis regarding a variation in the total quantity of primary material making up the planet—the state of the material in the Earth's **core** may be different to what traditional chemistry would suggest. The magma emerging along the ocean ridges

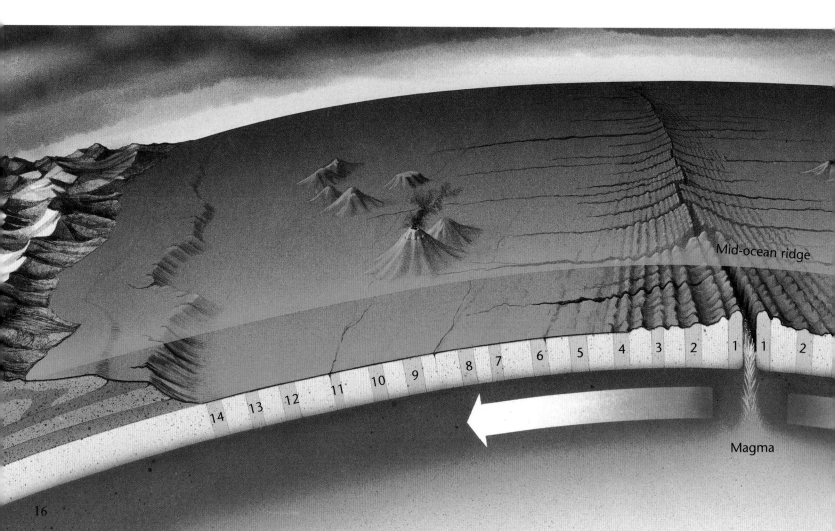

ay have a new form of chemical struc-
re that has its origins in a substratum of
batomic particles. The physical proper-
s (volume, mass, gravity, etc.) of these
rticles may be very different to those of
aterial produced through their combina-
on. The variation in the state of the mate-
l could result in an increase in the
mensions of the planet.

Today it is thought that the diameter of
e Earth was little over half the size of its
rrent average diameter 700 million
ars ago. The British geologist Hugh G.
wen says that the South American and
rican continents fit together perfectly, in
cordance with their geological similari-
s, if we assume that the diameter of the
rth was 80% of the current diameter of
rth 190-200 million years ago. This the-
y also works when we fit together the
ntinents bordering the Arctic, Indian,
d North Atlantic oceans.

Left: The expansion of the ocean floors.
The magma from the mantle emerges
from the ocean ridges and spreads either
side of the ridge. This means that the
magnetic characteristics of the rock in the
ocean floor—aligned according to the
direction of the Earth's magnetic field at
the moment in which the magma
solidifies—will be identical on either side
of the ridge and will be arranged in
symmetrical bands (numbered in the
diagram) parallel to the ridge.

Below: a) A simulation of the fit of South
America with Africa with the Earth at its
current size; the red areas indicate gaps.
b) The same simulation with the diameter
of the Earth equal to 80% of its current
size, in agreement with all the geological
data.

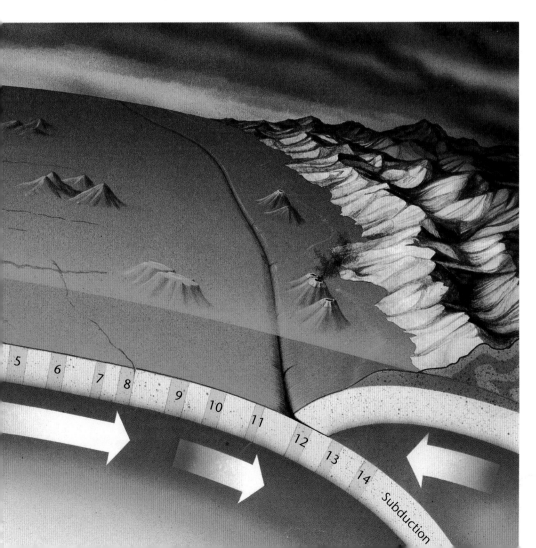

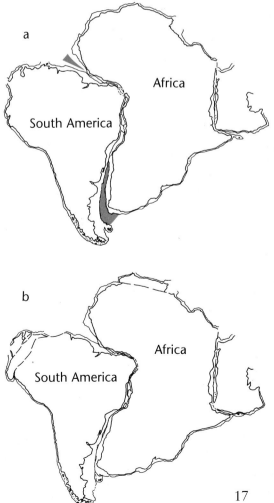

SEDIMENTS

The ocean floor is thickly covered with **sediments**. These can be divided into two groups—terrigenous sediments and pelagic sediments.

The terrigenous sediments come from dry land and consist of **sand, silt,** and **clay.** The largest grains are deposited close to the coast, with the finer grains being deposited progressively farther out to sea.

The pelagic sediments consist mainly of the shells of organisms and mineral residues produced by the decomposition of organisms. Occasionally elements of cosmic origin (meteorite dust) and volcanic ashes may be found in the pelagic sediments. The cosmic dusts are deposited and aligned according to the direction of the Earth's magnetic field. Since each position of the magnetic field corresponds to a precise period, these dusts are very useful in dating the strata.

The rate of growth of the sediment deposits is different in the various areas of the ocean floor. The coastal sediments are greatly influenced by the movement of the **tides** and currents and by climatic variations, and they grow at a variable, but relatively high, rate. The sediments on the deep-sea floor are deposited at a more regular, but extremely slow, rate—perhaps as slow as 2-3 centimeters (0.78-1.18 in) over thousands of years, or, in the case of red clays, hundreds of thousands of years.

The thickness of the sediment layer is also variable. It ranges from around 1,000 meters (3,280 ft) on the abyssal plains to 100-200 meters (328-656 ft) on the mid-ocean ridges and irregular floors in general. Close to the shore, the sediment layer is even thinner.

The components of the marine sediments are divided into lithogenic components (comprising quartz, mica, clay, and other rock derivatives), biogenic components (minerals derived from shells or parts of algae and organic material deriving from the partial decomposition of organic substances), and hydrogenic components (substances present in solution, together with the water trapped by the porosity of the sediments).

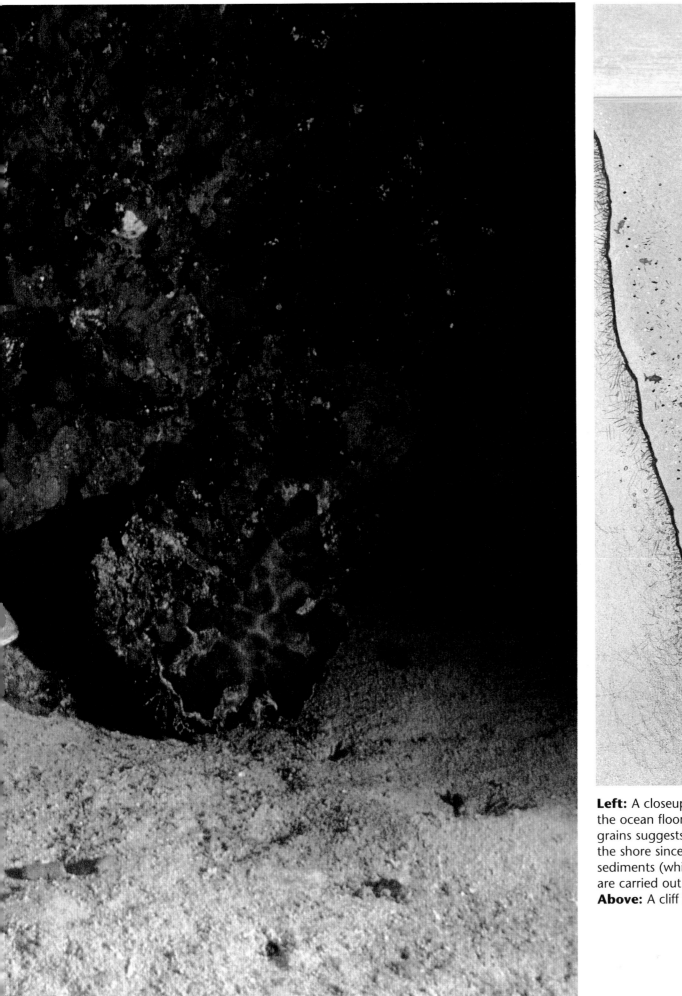

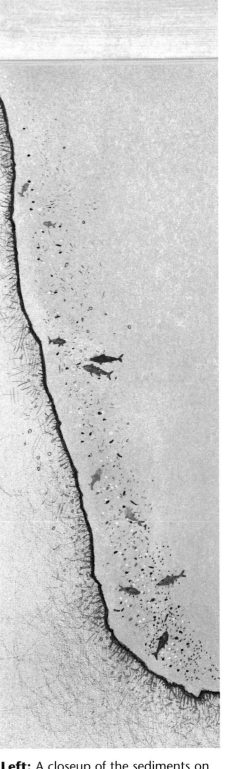

Left: A closeup of the sediments on the ocean floor. The large size of the grains suggests that we are close to the shore since only the finest sediments (which float more easily) are carried out to sea in suspension.
Above: A cliff in the intertidal zone.

The oceans are constantly moving. Leaving aside the possible causes, this phenomenon is important because it influences the lives of the marine plants and animals. One of the movements most typical of the ocean waters is the one that results in the formation of waves.

It is almost always the movement of the air (i.e., the wind) acting on the surface of the ocean that provides the thrust that sets the water in motion with a mechanical energy that generates waves. The formation of the waves may also depend on other factors like landslides or undersea earthquakes, but these are not very frequent.

Waves normally develop on the surface, at the point of contact between the air and the water. A wave's size depends on three factors—the duration of the contact between the air and the water, the speed of the wind, and the size of the area of water with which the wind comes into contact.

The waves do not carry the water with them, but instead make it move "on the spot." The water actually circulates in short elliptical patterns. What is transmitted, at times over long distances, is the energy generated by the movements of the water particles. The fact that the motion of these water particles follows an elliptical pattern determines the "shape" of the waves. The upper part of a wave is known as the crest, and the lower part is called the trough. The distance between two successive crests gives the wave length, and the vertical distance between the upper tip of the crest and the base of the trough gives the wave height.

There are various types of wave that depend on the strength of the wind generating them. Light breezes generate the formation of surface ripples just a few millimeters high and a few centimeters long. These ripples are known as surface waves. If the strength of the wind increases, the length and height of the waves will also increase. In this case the waves are known as gravitational waves. Lastly, when the wind is fairly strong, the waves begin to "roll," moving away from the wind that generated them. In this case the crests of

Above: As they approach the coast from the open sea, waves increase in height.
Right: A diagram of the movement of water particles within a wave: their orbital motion is responsible for the shape of the wave. The particles follow an elliptical orbit from the surface toward the sea floor. The greater the depth of the water, the smaller the waves.

Direction of the wave ⟶

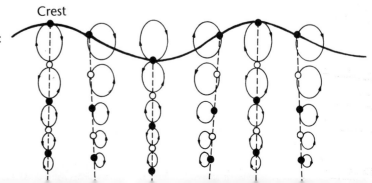
Crest

the waves become rounded and become swells, capable of traveling for thousands of kilometers. When the waves approach the coast, they change shape. In shallow waters, the water particles in motion strike the seabed. The consequent **friction** causes the wavelength to diminish and the wave height to increase. Friction also reduces the speed of the waves. When the water is too shallow, the waves can no longer hold their shape, and they consequently break onto the beach.

All coastal marine life is affected by the motion of the waves and has had to adapt accordingly. In general, marine organisms are particularly abundant in estuaries, lagoons, and protected bays, and are much

less numerous along the beaches and rocky coasts.

One very unusual type of wave is the **tsunami**. This vast wave is generated by earthquakes or the eruption of an underwater volcano. The shaking of the ocean floor transmits an enormous quantity of energy to the water, generating a huge wave which may be over 150 kilometers (93 mi) long and capable of traveling for hours (and hundreds of kilometers) before breaking on the shore with devastating violence.

Below: Waves breaking on the beach.
Bottom: A diagram showing how a wave breaks as it approaches the shore. Friction against the seabed changes the shape of the wave. When the depth of the water is half the length of the wave, friction slows the wave and causes it to increase in weight. When the depth of the water is less than half the length of the wave, the wave breaks on the shore.

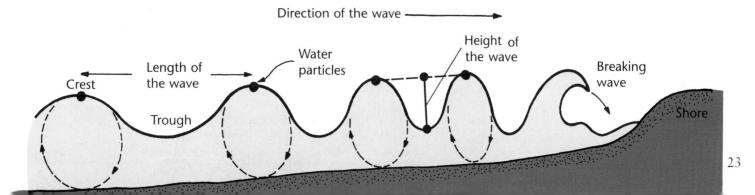

Direction of the wave ⟶

Water particles

Height of the wave

Length of the wave

Breaking wave

Crest

Trough

Shore

MOVEMENT: CURRENTS

A Planetary System

Waves are not the only factor contributing to the constant motion of the ocean. Currents are also of fundamental importance. Currents are rivers of water with homogeneous temperature, **salinity**, and density characteristics that flow through the oceans.

Currents may be caused by differences in the salinity or temperature of the water or, like waves, by the action of the wind. Currents are particularly linked to constant winds like the **trade winds**. Winds are responsible for the creation of a complex system of surface currents known as drift currents. The drift currents form inlets and meanders, and in each ocean basin they give rise to great gyres connected by linking currents.

The Earth is constantly moving through space, and this movement is responsible for a force that deflects currents in the Northern Hemisphere to the right, and those in the Southern Hemisphere to the left. This deflection of the currents is called the **Coriolis Effect**. As a result, the water at the surface of the oceans in the Northern Hemisphere slowly spins in a clockwise direction. In the Southern Hemisphere, the water spins in a counterclockwise direction. At the equator the two deflections are balanced out, and both the winds and the ocean currents can move in a straight line.

Gradient Currents and Upwelling

The other important factor in the creation of horizontal or vertical ocean currents is represented by variations in the density of the water. All currents provoked by differences in water density, whether surface, deep, horizontal, or vertical currents, are known as gradient currents. The classic example of a surface gradient current is the famous Gulf Stream. This current is formed in the Gulf of Mexico, then enters the Atlantic Ocean between Florida and Cuba, and eventually flows past the northwestern coasts of Europe.

Density of sea water depends on two main factors—temperature and salinity. A third factor, pressure, comes into play at great depths. Water temperature and salinity depend in turn on external factors such as changes in atmospheric temperature, the amount of sunlight that hits the water, and all the factors that may cause the water to freeze or to evaporate. Both freezing and evaporation remove water from the sea, increasing the salinity of the remaining water while lowering its temperature at the same time. This process leads to an increase in water density. When the water at the surface becomes denser than the water below it, there is vertical movement because the surface water will then sink to the bottom.

Upwellings are rising currents of water and are extremely important for marine life. The water at the surface of the sea is warmer and poorer in nutrients due to the continual consumption by marine organisms. Currents take this surface water away from the coasts and allow the denser and colder water to rise from the depths. This water is richer in dissolved nutrients. The upwelling of water from the bottom of the sea brings **nitrates** and phosphates

Below: A map of the surface currents in the world's oceans.
Top right: An example of a subsurface or "thermosaline" current in the Atlantic. The salty, cold, polar water descends toward the ocean floor (because of its high density) and flows slowly toward the equator. The bottom waters of Antarctic origin are even denser than the Arctic waters and therefore lie even deeper.
Bottom right: A map of the major coastal upwellings and the prevailing winds that produce them.

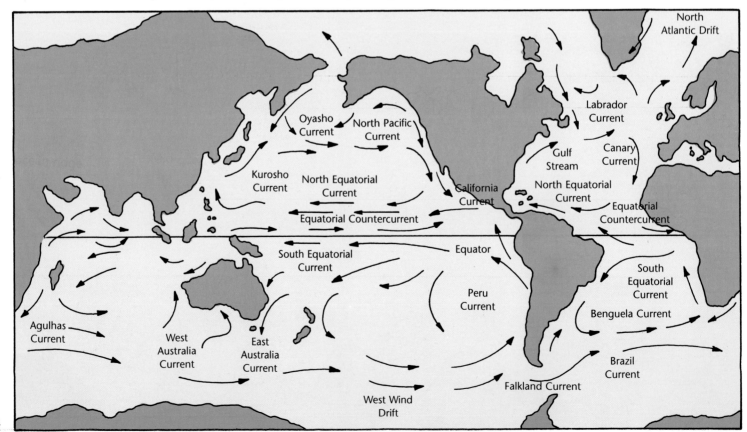

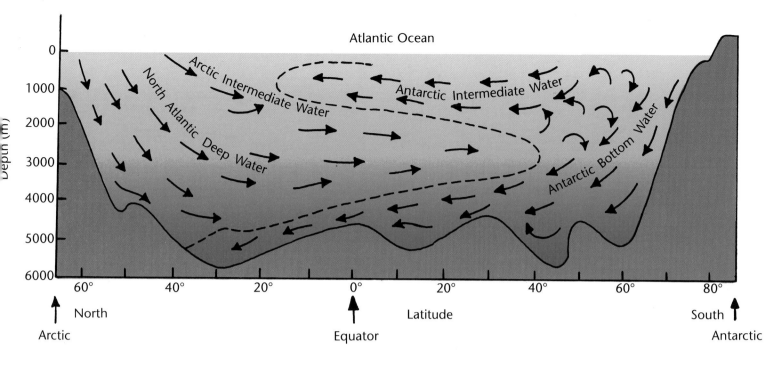

to the surface. These substances are vital to the plants floating on the surface and therefore to the animals feeding on the plants.

A number of human activities, fishing above all, depend on this process. It is well known, for example, that anchovy fishing off the South American coast is thrown into crisis when a change in the direction of the wind interrupts the upwelling that is typical of the region.

In the major oceans, we can identify three layers below the surface water. Each of these layers has its own temperature and salinity characteristics. The first layer is known as the intermediate water and is characterized by a low level of salinity.

Below this layer is the deep-water layer that originates in the North Atlantic with a high degree of salinity. This layer extends to a depth of almost 2,000 meters (6,562 ft). Lastly, toward the sea floor, there is the very dense bottom water originating in the Antarctic. This cold water spreads along the bottoms of the oceans at depths of up to 4,000 meters (13,124 ft).

This structure creates what are called subsurface currents—also known as thermosaline currents because their movement depends on differences in temperature and salinity—that allow great quantities of dissolved oxygen to reach the organisms living in the ocean depths. Without this oxy-

gen, life at the bottom of the oceans would not exist.

Subsurface and surface currents are also responsible for the dispersal of the eggs of organisms living in deep water. Without these currents, the organisms would have difficulty colonizing new areas of the sea bed. Finally, the movement of the currents in general carries the heat accumulated in the waters of the equatorial regions toward the poles. At the same time, the frigid polar water is carried toward the tropics, thus regulating the climate throughout the ocean regions.

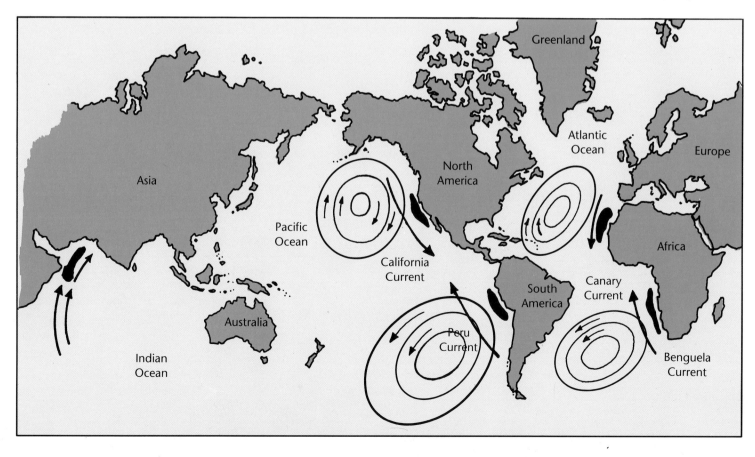

The movement of
a subsurface current.

MOVEMENT: TIDES

Rhythms of Activity and Repose

final type of movement of sea water is
movement. Tidal movement is the peri-
raising and lowering of the level of the
it affects all of the world's coastlines.
have a profound effect on the marine
nisms living along the shore. These
nisms are periodically exposed to the

dangers of drying out when the retreating
tide leaves them exposed. There also is the
threat of inundation when the advancing
tide covers them again. Since the tides affect
that part of the sea richest in life—the entire
coastline—the coastal organisms have adapted to cope with them. They are even able to
exploit the rhythms of the sea to fit in with

their own periods of intense activity and
periods of repose. Along the ocean coasts,
low tide could represent the beginning of an
immense disaster if—for some obscure reason—it should be prolonged beyond the
usual time. In reality that can never happen,
and the myriad organisms temporarily
exposed to the air have only a few hours to

wait before they are returned to their oxygen-rich marine environment.

The Effect of the Moon

Tides are, in effect, extremely long waves moving across the oceans. High tide occurs when an area of coast is reached by the crest (highest point) of this wave, and low tide occurs when the coast is reached by the trough (lowest point). These extremely long waves are a direct product of the gravitational pull between the Earth and the moon.

This gravitational pull effectively causes the formation of two enormous bulges. One is on the side of Earth facing the moon, with the other on the opposite side.

The two photos show the beach and the port at Saint-Malò, in France, at high and low tide. All the marine organisms are directly or indirectly influenced by the rhythms of the sea and must adapt accordingly. Man is also influenced by these rhythms when planning his navigational and fishing activities.

The first is a consequence of the reciprocal attraction between the Earth and the moon. The water is, so to speak, "lifted" by the moon's gravity. The second bulge, on the other hand, is produced by the centrifugal force created as the Earth and the moon orbit a common point called the **barycenter**, or, center of gravity.

As the Earth and moon orbit each other, the centrifugal force on this side of the Earth created by their movement is sufficient to overcome their combined gravitational pull. There is again a "lifting" of the water, but in the opposite direction to the first. These two bulges inevitably cause a lowering of the sea level on the other two faces of the Earth. If the Earth was completely covered with water, and if the duration of the rotation of the Earth-moon system was the same as that of the rotation of the Earth on its axis, the high and low tides would alternate with absolute precision every six hours during the day. In reality the tides occur at different times each day. This is due to various factors, above all as a consequence of the relative movements of the Earth and the moon, and of both with respect to the sun.

The moon completes an apparent revolution around the Earth in 24 hours and 50 minutes, also known as a lunar day. Therefore the moon changes its position in the sky within the 24 hours that the Earth takes to complete a revolution on its axis. As the moon orbits the Earth, it appears 50 minutes later each day. As a consequence of this, the tides also occur 50 minutes later each day. Therefore there are 12 hours and 25 minutes between successive high tides, which are usually called semidiurnal tides.

The Contribution of the Sun

In many coastal areas, the tidal range—the difference in height between the high and low tides—changes day by day. These variations are directly linked to the gravitational pull of the sun and the moon. The tides provoked by the sun are half as strong as those caused by the moon. Even though the sun is much larger than the moon, it is so much farther from the Earth that its gravitational pull is weaker. The strongest tides occur when the Earth, the sun, and the moon are aligned and their respective forces of gravity are combined. This alignment occurs twice every lunar month (approximately 29 and a half days), the time taken by the moon to complete a revolution about the Earth. To be precise, these tides coincide with the appearance of the new moon and the full moon. In contrast, the tides are weakest when the sun and the moon are at a right angle compared with the Earth.

The orbit of the Earth and the moon on a common point, 4,670 kilometers (2,902 miles) from the center of the Earth, gives rise to the tides on opposite sides of the Earth due to the gravitational pull on the side facing the moon and due to the centrifugal force generated by the rotation on the other side.

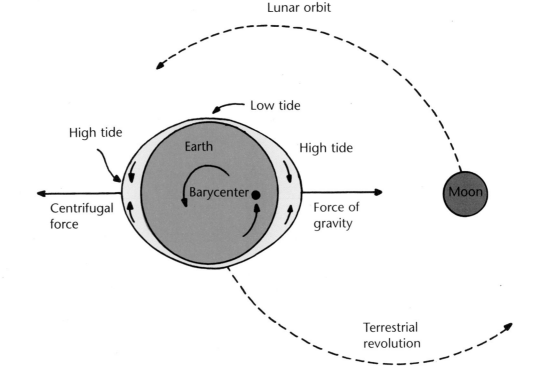

THE LEVEL OF THE SEA

It is believed that the total volume of water to be found on the Earth during the various geological eras has never changed significantly. However this does not mean that the level of the sea was also constant. On the contrary, throughout geological time there have been notable and even radical changes to the level of the sea. As a consequence of these changes, the coastlines have also been subjected to radical modifications.

From this point of view, one of the most important and dramatic periods was during the relatively recent Pleistocene, occurring within the last two million years. During this period the level of the sea changed drastically due to the formation (and subsequent melting) of the great continental glaciers during the four major ice advances (the Günz, Mindel, Riss, and Würm). In all four cases, the level of the sea was significantly lowered because so much water was frozen and therefore trapped in its solid state. When the glaciers were at their peak, the level of the sea was no less than 150 meters (492 ft) lower than it is now. This means that much of the continental shelf was exposed to erosion by rivers. Traces of this process can still be seen clearly.

Just 15,000 years ago, the level of the sea was still about 120 meters (394 ft) lower than it is today. From then until about 3,000 years ago, it rose relatively rapidly because the glaciers melted. The water covered the continental shelf and transformed the canyons eroded by the rivers into great submarine valleys.

A Slow, Constant Increase

3,000 years ago the rate of the rise in the level of the sea slowed considerably. From that point on, the increase has continued, but it has been slow and irregular (with an increase of about 10 meters [33 ft] over the last 3,000 years). Nevertheless, the level of the sea continues to rise even though the great continental glaciers have melted. Many scientists believe that this is being caused by a progressive rise in the temperature of the Earth (partly caused by the so-called **greenhouse effect**) which in turn is causing the polar ice caps to melt, thus increasing the volume of water in the oceans. What is certain is that many currently dry coastal areas may very well become submerged if the rise continues.

Right: Steep rocks on the Paracas Peninsula in Peru.

Below: A diagram of the changes in the profile of the Atlantic coast near Baltimore over the last 15,000 years. Since the last glaciation—during which it was lowered by 120 meters (394 ft)—the level of the sea has continued to rise. The diagram shows the coastline as it may appear in the future if the polar ice caps melt completely.

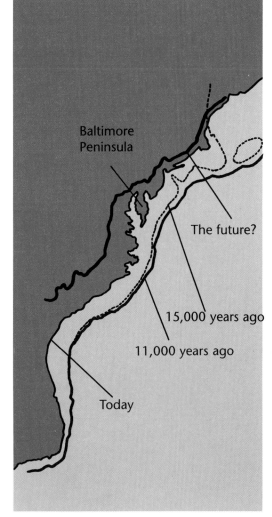

Baltimore Peninsula

The future?

15,000 years ago

11,000 years ago

Today

Temperature, Light, and Sound

Temperature

The temperature of the water is one of the most important physical factors in the marine environment. It determines and limits the distribution of organisms in the oceans. It also influences the density of the water, its degree of salinity, and the quantity of dissolved gases found within it.

Temperature normally varies according to latitude. The imaginary lines that link the various points in the oceans with identical temperatures (isotherms) have a pattern similar to those of the parallels of latitude. In the temperate regions, the isotherms are subjected to seasonal variations, while in the polar and tropical seas the temperatures are much more stable.

The temperature of the sea is also influenced by the distance from the coast and the depth of the water. It gradually decreases and becomes more stable as you move from the surface toward the sea floor. In the deep-sea areas, the temperature is constant. The most notable variations in temperature are found in the **intertidal zones** and where warm and cold currents meet. The intertidal zones are regularly exposed by the tides and therefore absorb the heat of the sun differently.

The temperature of the water is also extremely important to marine organisms because it influences metabolic rates and reproductive cycles. Almost all marine animals and all marine plants are ectotherms. This means that their body temperature changes in relation to the ambient temperature of their environment. As their body temperature increases, the speed of the processes taking place within their bodies (their metabolism) also increases.

It should also be kept in mind that the higher the temperature of the water, the lower the quantity of dissolved oxygen the water contains. For this reason marine organisms adapted to cold, oxygen-rich waters risk suffocation if the temperature rises greatly.

Light

Another extremely important physical factor in the marine environment is sunlight. The penetration of the water by the sun's rays is a critical factor in the survival of marine organisms. Sunlight is vital for plants and phytoplankton if they are to complete the process of photosynthesis and produce the molecules of glucose that represent the basis of the entire food chain.

Most of the sunlight that reaches the oceans simply gets reflected back. Most of the relatively small percentage that actually penetrates the water is absorbed and transformed into heat and is therefore no longer available for photosynthesis. Almost 65% of the light is absorbed in this process in the first meter of water. Most marine organisms are concentrated in the area of the sea illuminated by the sun (known as the photic zone) even though this area accounts for less than 10% of the total volume of water covering the Earth.

An important physical property of sea water is that of absorbing the sun's rays in a selective manner according to their wavelengths. First the red and yellow waves that are most important for photosynthesis are absorbed. Then the shorter wavelengths like the blue and ultraviolet rays are absorbed. These may penetrate as deep as 500 meters (1,640 ft) beneath the surface.

Sound

One last important physical factor regarding sea water is its excellent capacity for transmitting sound waves. The speed of sound in water depends on temperature, salinity, and pressure. Therefore it is not constant at all depths and varies irregularly in the various seas and oceans.

Right: The intensity of light decreases as you descend toward the sea floor.
In the box: Sea water absorbs sunlight in a selective manner according to the wavelength of the rays. The red and yellow rays do not penetrate deeper than 200 meters (656 ft). The blue and ultraviolet rays with their shorter wavelengths may penetrate as deep as 500 meters (1,640 ft).

Sun

Red

Yellow

Blue

Ultraviolet rays

100

200

300

400

500

Meters

THE SEA AND THE ATMOSPHERE

The Greenhouse Effect

The sea and the atmosphere are both in constant motion, and they continually influence each other.

The first fundamental effect of the atmosphere on sea water is that it ensures that the water remains in a liquid state over almost all of the planet, making it habitable and inhabited. This is due to the so-called **greenhouse effect** whereby various gases, especially water vapor and **carbon dioxide**, "mist" the atmosphere and limit the dispersal of heat that the Earth accumulates from the sun's rays. Without the greenhouse effect, the average temperature on the surface of the Earth would be much lower: -15°C (5°F) rather than +15°C (59°F). The greenhouse effect is therefore responsible for keeping most of the water in a liquid state and restricting the ice caps to the polar regions. This allows the oceans to contribute to the absorption and storage of part of the sun's heat, therefore maintaining the optimum conditions for life on Earth. Currently, however, the release of carbon dioxide and other gases into the atmosphere by man is increasing the greenhouse effect to a potentially dangerous degree.

A Heat Store

The atmosphere can be seen as a kind of "heat machine" that transforms the energy it receives from the sun into mechanical energy to keep itself in motion.

The atmosphere absorbs heat energy close to the ground. Part of this heat energy is passed to the cooler upper layers of the atmosphere, and the rest is transformed into mechanical energy. Much of the necessary heat energy comes from the oceans. This happens in two ways—if a mass of cool air passes over an area of warmer water, there will be a direct exchange of heat from the water to the air. A second and more important process is the evaporation of the water that warms the air and cools the surface of the water. The sea's great capacity to absorb and then release heat means that it has a great influence over climate.

Compared with dry land, the temperature of the sea is less variable—it warms up more slowly in the summer and cools more slowly in the winter. Since water has a greater **thermal capacity** than air, the wind adapts to the temperature of the water when it blows over the sea, and not the other way around. This explains why maritime climates are much more stable and well-balanced than continental climates.

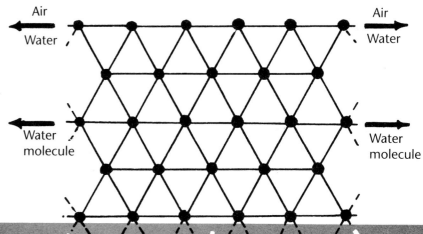

Below: The atmospheric system determines which areas and how much of the ocean are covered by cloud layers. This in turn determines the amount of solar heat they are capable of absorbing. On the other hand, the instability of this system ensures that all areas experience periods that are hotter or colder than normal.

Right: The high surface tension of the water is derived from the unbalanced forces of attraction between the individual molecules. The arrows show that the resulting forces are directed downward and sideways.

SALINITY

One of the fundamental chemical characteristics of sea water is its **salinity**. Rain, wind, submarine volcanic activity, and, above all, material washed down rivers and into the sea are constant sources of mineral salts. On the other hand, **salt** is extracted from sea water by sedimentation. The addition and subtraction of salt balances out, and the average salinity of the sea remains constant. The average saline concentration of the sea is equal to 34.7 parts salt to 1,000 parts water. In practical terms this means that, in a liter (0.26 gal) of sea water, 3.47% is salt and the remaining 96.53% is water.

Almost all the salt dissolved in sea water is composed of sodium, potassium, magnesium, bromides, fluorides, carbonates, and borates. The aforementioned 3.47% average salinity is usually found in open sea, in the centers of the great ocean basins. It is a different matter closer to the coasts, the river deltas, and in some internal seas.

The degree of salinity is not the same in all regions. The region between the tropics—which is subject to heavy evaporation—is the richest in salt. The degree of salinity decreases toward the poles. The continental seas that are surrounded by lands with a dry climate have an above-average degree of salinity. In some areas the salinity of the Mediterranean reaches 3.7% or even 3.8%, and that of the Red Sea reaches peaks of 4.5%. Seas surrounded by lands with wet climates and major rivers have lower salinity levels. In some areas of the Baltic, the degree of salinity is below 0.2%. Naturally the tidal zones and the river estuaries are also characterized by considerable variations in salinity.

If you examine a vertical column of water, you will see that salinity also varies in relation to depth. The water at the surface is constantly stirred by the wind, the tides, and the waves. Therefore its salinity is essentially uniform in spite of certain seasonal variations linked to atmospheric factors. Below the surface is a layer (that may reach depths of up to 500 meters [1,640 ft]) characterized by notable varia-

tions in the degree of salinity as the depth increases. Below this level, however, the salinity of the water is constant and remains so for thousands of meters.

Below: Around 6 million years ago, during the upper Miocene, the link between the Mediterranean and the Atlantic via the Strait of Gibraltar was interrupted. Over the course of a few hundred thousand years, the Mediterranean dried out due to the almost total evaporation of the water and had been transformed into an immense salt desert.
Facing page, bottom: A salt pan in Brittany, France.

SUBSTANCES FOR LIFE

Nitrogen

Sea water contains a number of dissolved gases. The most abundant of these is **nitrogen** (making up around 50% of the total dissolved gas). The nitrogen in sea water comes mainly from the atmosphere. Its concentration increases when the temperature and salinity of the water decreases. The nitrogen **atoms** are important components in the protein and amino-acid molecules that marine organisms need to make new tissues, like cell membranes, blood, skin, and scales. In order to form part of the organic molecules, the dissolved nitrogen has to undergo a process of transformation known as "fixing." This process is performed by bacteria and algae and involves the combination of inert nitrogen atoms with oxygen atoms.

Nutrient Salts

The nitrogen and the small quantities of **phosphorus** and **silicon** compounds found dissolved in sea water can be described as nutrient salts. All are of great importance to marine life because they form the basis for organic syntheses and other fundamental processes. These compounds are used in the upper layers of the sea, where photosynthesis takes place. When marine organisms die, their organic material decomposes and is deposited on the sea floor. The nutrient salt compounds are then reconstituted, mainly through the action of bacteria. The turbulence and the rising currents of the sea carry the compounds back to the upper layers, where they can be found in considerable concentrations. Nutrient salts are then ready to be reused by the marine organisms.

Carbon Dioxide

Carbon dioxide plays a fundamental role in photosynthesis. The carbon atoms are used to make complex organic compounds such as fats, sugars, and **proteins**, all of which are essential substances for plant and animal life. Carbon dioxide is highly soluble in water, and it has been calculated that there is 50% more carbon dioxide in the oceans than in the atmosphere. Most of the carbon dioxide in the sea is present in the form of calcium and magnesium carbonates. These substances are used in the formation of the shells of marine animals and are found in sediments. The concentration of carbon dioxide dissolved in sea water is usually fairly constant.

Marine pH

Reversible chemical reactions occur between sea water and carbon dioxide. These reactions allow the carbon dioxide to pass into the atmosphere and into the cells of plants through diffusion. The same reactions also permit the concentration of hydrogen atoms in the sea to be regulated. This concentration is usually expressed as a **pH** value.

The pH value scale ranges from 0 to 14 and represents the changed sign logarithm of the hydrogen ions ($pH = -\log[H+L]$). A pH value of 7 is neutral, with values below 7 being acidic and values above 7 being alkaline.

Below: These nitrogenous compounds are derived from the decomposition of animals and plants—calcium carbonates in the bones, shells, and corals; silicates in the corals and siliceous sponges; and phosphates in many varieties as with the other compounds.
Right: The structure of silicon and cyclosilicate crystals.

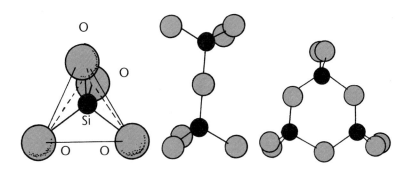

PROPERTIES OF SEA WATER

An Unusual Molecule

We are now going to examine the nature and properties of the principal substance composing the sea—water.

The molecular structure of water makes it a truly unique chemical compound, with properties that permit the existence of life. Water molecules are composed of two hydrogen atoms and one oxygen atom. Each hydrogen atom shares an **electron** with the oxygen atom. This shared electron creates links that bind each water molecule together.

Water molecules are also characterized by an asymmetrical distribution of their electrical charge. This means that the shared electrons are shifted toward the oxygen atom (due to the characteristics of

ly charged oxygen atom at the opposite extremity of a neighboring molecule.

In this way, bonds like bridges are formed between one water molecule and another. These bonds are capable of linking the water molecules together in a vast web. Without these bonds water would already be a gas at temperatures as low as -80°C (-112°F). Instead water boils at 100°C (212°F), and the oceans exist in liquid form. As the temperature of water rises, there are fewer hydrogen bonds, and the movement of its molecules increases. This influences both the movement of the water itself and that of the various organisms swimming through it. The "resistance" of water to flow, or its **viscosity**, is in fact directly linked to the number of

example, the plankton drifting in the fairly cold, and therefore highly viscous, waters of the oceans need to expend only a minimum of energy in order to stay afloat. In contrast, the animals that have to swim though this same water will expend a great deal of energy because of its high viscosity.

Surface tension also has importance from the point of view of movement, especially of waves. Surface tension is influenced by temperature and salinity and ultimately by the reciprocal attraction of the water molecules that result from the hydrogen bonds. This attraction is in fact unbalanced and provokes a kind of "strain" of the surface of the water and the creation of a kind of very thin film. This high surface tension determines the

Left: Five water molecules linked by hydrogen bonds represented by lines. These bonds are responsible for many of the water's unusual properties; its high boiling point, for example.

Below: The greenhouse effect may increase temperatures in the Mediterranean by two degrees during the winter and two to four degrees during the summer. In northern Europe the increase would be six degrees during the winter and two degrees during the summer.

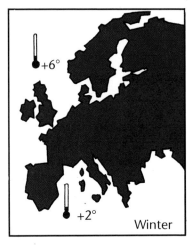

Winter

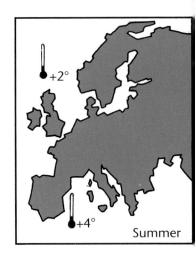

Summer

oxygen compared with those of hydrogen). Consequently the oxygen atom has a negative charge compared with the other side of the molecule with the two hydrogen atoms. This characteristic means that water molecules are polarized, and the main effect of this **polarization** is that water molecules attract each other. More precisely, the positively charged extremity of each molecule corresponds to a hydrogen atom and is attracted by the negative-

hydrogen bonds within its molecular structure. It is influenced in part by the salinity of the water (a high level of salinity leads to a slightly higher viscosity) and to a large degree by its temperature (the higher the temperature, the lower the viscosity of the water).

Viscosity, Surface Tension, and Density

The viscosity of water has an important effect on the lives of marine organisms. For example, the plankton drifting in the fairly

existence of a sharply defined confine between water and air.

The strength of the surface tension increases when the temperature decreases and the number of hydrogen bonds increases. The "integrity" of the surface of the water is important for the survival of many organisms—not only those rare insects that live on the surface, but also numerous other organisms, such as bacteria, protozoa, fish eggs or fish larvae, and even some species of jellyfish.

The elevated density of sea water helps to support marine organisms. This means that it is a comfortable environment even for huge animals, like whales. The hydrogen bonds, together with changes in temperature, also have a great influence on the density of the water. When the water cools, the movement of the molecules slows due to the formation of more hydrogen bonds. This means that, in a certain

Thermal Capacity

Water also has an elevated capacity for absorbing heat (**thermal capacity**). This allows it to resist rapid changes in atmospheric temperature, ensuring that the marine environment is very stable and that any changes are gradual.

Much of the solar heat that reaches the Earth is absorbed by the oceans. However, the temperature of the oceans does not constantly increase as the water is cooled

The transfer of heat to the interior of the oceans, on the other hand, depends largely on the water movements that are caused by differences in density (subsurface currents).

A Universal Solvent

Another fundamental property of water is that it is a virtually universal solvent of polarized substances (which in itself is a vast category of materials). When water

Water molecules are composed of two hydrogen atoms (H) and one oxygen atom (O). When they combine they produce energy (E).

sense, the molecules are more tightly "packed" and the water is denser. Below a certain temperature, however, the density of the water diminishes, and when it freezes, the formation of ice crystals increases its volume and at the same time separates the water molecules. As a consequence, the mass/volume ratio decreases along with the water density. Ice is, in fact, less dense than water, which is why it floats.

by surface evaporation. This releases heat and water vapor into the atmosphere. Evaporation plays an important role in regulating the internal temperature of organisms living in the tidal zone. For example, the plants growing on the coasts eliminate excess heat by allowing part of the water content to evaporate through their leaves. A similar system is used by mussels, which open slightly to allow water to evaporate.

molecules come into contact with salt crystals, the crystals break up, dissociating into ions (negatively or positively charged particles) of chloride and sodium. The negatively charged oxygen atom in each water molecule attracts the sodium ions with a positive charge, and the positively charged hydrogen atoms attract the negatively charged chloride atoms. The ions are covered with a "film" of water that keeps the salt dissolved. This process is called hydration. Substances like proteins and **amino acids**, which do not separate into ions, can also be dissolved in water.

Sea water contains almost all the known natural elements and has a series of particularly important components. These principal components do not vary significantly in terms of type or quantity in the various oceans of the world, mainly because the waters of the oceans are constantly circulating and mixing. This compositional stability is called the "principal of constant proportions." Various sources, river outlets above all, constantly add new substances to sea water. At the same time, however, other substances are removed by the effects of the wind and waves or because they are incorporated into the shells of marine organisms (e.g., calcium and silicon) or become trapped in sediment by a series of chemical reactions. Because of all this, the addition and subtraction of substances to and from the water is balanced out.

Vapor

Water

The three physical states of water. From top to bottom: GAS, LIQUID, and SOLID, and their corresponding molecular structures (light gray—oxygen; dark gray—hydrogen; dotted line—hydrogen bond).
In the case of VAPOR, all the molecules are free of hydrogen bonds and act as independent entities. In the case of liquid (WATER), some molecules are linked by hydrogen bonds while others are free.
In the case of ICE, each water molecule is linked by hydrogen bonds, forming a reticulate crystalline structure.

Ice

THE ORIGINS OF LIFE

Self-replicating Molecules

The sea was the cradle of life. It was here that life originated and subsequently developed and spread throughout the oceans and then onto dry land. How could such a remarkable event have happened? And what exactly is life?

A biologist would probably give an indirect answer to these questions. For example, he or she might say that the material and the energy present in the universe may present a more or less complex organization. The biologist might also point out that, in nature, there are processes of decomposition that take place with a reduction of free energy and an increase in disorder. On the other hand, there are also processes of biosynthesis that take place with increases in free energy and decreases in disorder. In effect, if there is a universal quality to all forms of life, then it is the capacity to use energy to duplicate complex structures.

Since the essence of life is the capacity for self-replication, any questions about the origins of life hinge on a question as to the origins of self-replication. At this point it becomes clear that the smallest natural entity capable of self-replication is not the cell (which is an extraordinarily complex structure), but rather the chains of **nucleic acids** containing genetic information in the form of DNA (deoxyribonucleic acid) or RNA (ribonucleic acid).

We can assume that the earliest chains of nucleic acids were formed because of a simple chemical reaction that was repeated in the coastal pools—the polymeriza-tion of the **nucleotides,** which are the elementary units that make up the nucleic acids. The nucleotides themselves were formed through chemical synthesis, beginning with very simple substances—bases, phosphoric acid, and the sugar ribose. It is well known that one base, **adenine,** can easily be formed from hydrocyanic acid, itself produced from the reaction between **ammonia** and **carbon monoxide** (both of which were normal components of the Earth's atmosphere billions of years ago). As early as the 1930s, biologists Alexander Oparin and J. B. Haldane hypothesized that the atmosphere of the primordial Earth was similar to that of modern-day Jupiter or Saturn, i.e., it contained very little oxygen but was rich in hydrogen, methane, and ammonia.

Life Without Proteins?

Today the principal hypothesis that researchers are following is that the formation of self-replicating RNA was the crucial event that gave rise to living organisms, around four billion years ago. This hypothesis received a significant boost in 1983 following Thomas Cech and Sydney Altman's discovery of the so-called ribozymes (enzymes composed of RNA).

Before this discovery, only proteinic enzymes were known. And since these enzymes are biological catalysts *par excellence,* the scientists had previously been unable to understand how RNA could replicate itself before the appearance of proteins.

The ribozymes capable of catalyzing the "cutting" and "pasting" of pieces of pre-existing RNA now provided a window into a primordial world, where various pieces of RNA could have been competing to reproduce themselves. Each chain tended to destroy differing chains and use the pieces obtained from the demolition for self-replication. We can now assume that the chains of RNA can actually carry out such operations with a set of ribozymes.

Today the chains of nucleic acids still compete between themselves, but they do so in an exclusively indirect manner. They produce proteins that are used as weapons during the process we call "natural selection." We can think of the enzymatic proteins as offensive weapons, and the structural proteins as defensive shields.

Further research suggests that primitive RNA may have been capable of evolving. The American biologist Sol Spiegemann has succeeded in obtaining RNA that resists the destructive action of ribonuclease by repeatedly replicating itself in this enzyme's presence. The **evolution** of primitive RNA was probably the fundamental event in the development of life. It may have led to the synthesis of proteins, the formation of DNA, and the appearance of cells as the fundamental units of protection and cultivation of the chains of nucleic acids and proteins.

A Universal Protein

All this probably happened around four billion years ago in the sea, or rather in the warm shallow waters of the rock pools where the mineral substances that could act as catalysts for the delicate polymerization of the nucleotides could accumulate. This is the opinion shared by most biologists.

There are, however, those who have suggested that the fundamental molecules of life were produced away from the Earth and arrived from space. This hypothesis does not question the chemical processes described above but instead simply locates them elsewhere.

British cosmologist Fred Hoyle has pointed out that the average temperature in the central regions of a molecular cloud like the Orion Nebula is fairly close to that of the Earth's surface, and that the amount of material in the cloud is much greater than that present on the Earth. Therefore, according to Hoyle, it is possible that life could have originated in the galaxy and been present in all the molecular clouds. The earliest life forms could then have produced a quantity of genetic material much greater than any the Earth was capable of creating. This material could have been dispersed throughout the galaxy, meaning the Earth represents only one of the many sites of this widespread dispersal.

Genial intuition or overheated imagination? At the moment no one is capable of providing a definite answer. But we have fairly reliable information on the molecular mechanisms of the origin of life—wherever it took place—and it may well represent a universal process of transformation and organization of matter.

The great majority of scientists believe that the sea was the cradle of life.

Left: According to the French biologist Antoine Danchin, the chemical reaction that gave rise to life took place on rocks rather than in the sea.
Below: British cosmologist Fred Hoyle claims that life could have originated in space within the great molecular clouds, like the Orion Nebula seen here. Within these clouds there was not only a suitable temperature, but also organic molecules in much greater quantities than any found on Earth.
Facing page: A simplified diagram of the environmental conditions that probably led to the origin of life.

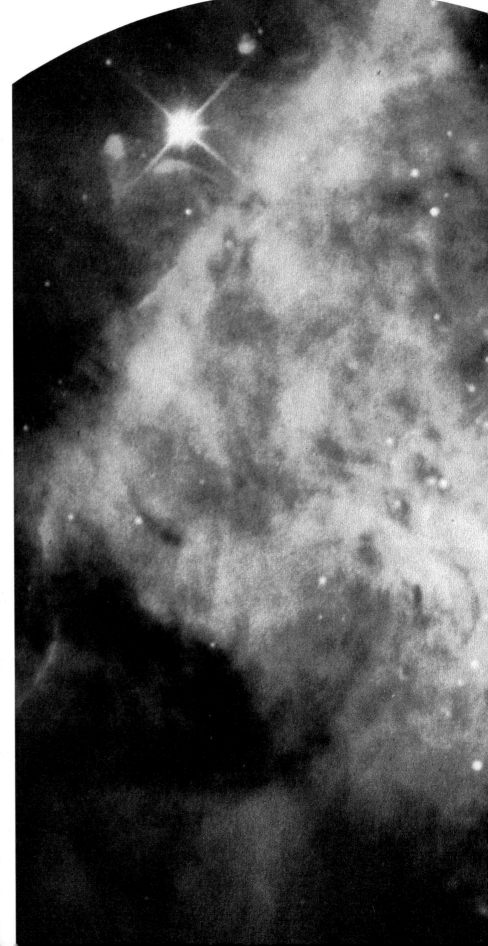

Ultraviolet radiation from the sun

Methane, ammonia, and water molecules

Rays from radioactive rocks

Amino acids forming in the water.

47

GLOSSARY

Words in *italics* can be found elsewhere in the glossary.

Abyssal plain Vast, relatively flat (slopes of less than 1/1000) expanses of *deep-sea floor* found at depths of between 1,000 and 6,000 meters (3,280 and 19,685 ft).

Adenine One of the four bases constituting the basic *nucleotides* of DNA (the others are thymine, guanine, and cytosine).

Amino acids Organic substances containing *nitrogen* that give rise to *proteins* by joining together in long chains.

Ammonia A chemical compound composed of a *nitrogen atom* and three oxygen *atoms*. It is present in the atmospheres of Jupiter and Saturn and was present in the Earth's atmosphere before the origin of life.

Asthenosphere The external part of the Earth's *mantle*, lying below the *crust*. It lies about 2,900 kilometers (1,802 mi) below the surface and continues on for about 100 to 400 kilometers (62 to 248 mi). It is composed of liquid rock (*magma*).

Atom The basic unit of matter. An atom is composed of a nucleus of positively charged protons and neutrons around which move a number of *electrons* (with a negative electric charge) equal to the number of protons.

Barycenter The center of gravity of a body or a system of bodies that are subject to reciprocal attraction.

Carbon dioxide A chemical compound composed of a carbon *atom* and two oxygen *atoms*. It represents the end product of the combustion of organic substances and the respiration of living things. It is the indispensable basis for the formation of calcium carbonate in rocks and in the shells of organisms.

Carbon monoxide A highly toxic gaseous compound composed of one carbon and one oxygen *atom*. It derives from the incomplete combustion of organic substances.

Circumpolar currents The circular movement of water around Antarctica caused by the merging currents arriving from the Atlantic, Pacific, and Indian Oceans. In the Northern Hemisphere, the land masses of Eurasia and North America prevent a similar Arctic current from forming.

Clay A silicic *sediment* composed of particles with diameters of less than 0.625 centimeters (0.246 in).

Continental margin The underwater portions of the *continental plates*, including the shallow *continental shelf*, the steep *continental slope*, and the gently sloping *continental rise*.

Continental plates The adjacent sections into which the Earth's *crust* is divided. Since they float on the fluid *asthenosphere*, they move slowly and continually with respect to one another. When they move apart, a margin results, and *magma* from the *asthenosphere* rises to form the *mid-ocean ridges*. When the plates collide, a destructive margin is formed and one of the plates subducts (moves under) the *asthenosphere*, forming a *deep-sea trench*.

Continental rise A fairly gentle slope that links the *continental slope* and the *abyssal plain*. It is formed by the *sediments* that descend from the *continental slope*.

Continental shelf The shallowest part of the *continental margin*. The continental shelf extends from the coastline to the edge of the *continental slope* at a depth of between 0 and 200 meters (0 and 656 ft) for about 70 kilometers (43 mi), although this is highly variable. It has a slope of between 1/500 and 1/1,000.

Continental slope The steeply sloping part of the *continental margin*.

Convective currents Slow rotational movements in a fluid caused by differences in *density*. The convective currents in the *asthenosphere* are formed because the deep-lying *magma* is warmer and less dense than it is at the surface. The less-dense magma tends to rise while the cooler, denser *magma* tends to sink.

Core The innermost part of the planet, lying below the *mantle*. The Earth's core has a radius of about 2,900 kilometers (1,802 mi).

It is thought to be composed of nickel and iron. The outer layer is probably fluid, and the inner section, which is subjected to incredibly high pressures, is probably solid.

Coriolis Effect The tendency for a *current* of water or air to turn to the right in the Northern Hemisphere and to the left in the Southern Hemisphere due to the effect of the Earth's rotation.

Crust The solid external shell of the Earth that floats on the *mantle*. It is mainly composed of light elements (*silicon*, aluminum, etc.). From a cross-section perspective of the Earth, the crust is thickest where the continents lay, and thinnest along the ocean floor. Its average thickness is around 40 kilometers (25 mi).

Deep-sea floor The part of the sea bed that extends between the margins of two *continental plates*. These include an *abyssal plain* and a *mid-ocean ridge* or *deep-sea trench*.

Deep-sea trench A long and deep underwater trough created at the point where the edge of a *continental plate* is *subducted* into the *asthenosphere*. The deepest one known is the Mariana Trench (11,022 meters [36,161 ft]).

Density The quantity of matter per unit of volume of a given substance compared with that of water. From a dimensional point of view, it is a pure number and therefore is conceptually different to the specific weight of a substance that is the weight (the force of gravity) of a given volume of a given substance.

Electron A subatomic particle with a negative charge and negligible mass that moves around the nucleus of the *atom*.

Equatorial current An ocean current produced by the *trade winds*. Like the trade winds, it moves from east to west, from the tropics to the Equator. The **equatorial countercurrent**, as its name implies, moves in the opposite direction (west to east).

Evolution A genetic change in a group of living things. Genes, composed of DNA, program the *proteins* and therefore the phenotypic characteristics of an organism. For each characteristic there are a number of possible alternative genes (alleles) present, in different frequencies, in each population. The variation of these frequencies may, very gradually, give rise to significant morphological changes, and this is the process of evolution.

Friction A force that opposes the relative movement of two touching bodies. The energy liberated from friction is transformed into heat.

Greenhouse Effect The heating of the Earth due to the atmosphere's capacity for absorbing heat and trapping it in the same way that panes of glass in a greenhouse trap heat (hence the name "greenhouse" effect). The degree of absorption depends on the quantities of certain gases (e.g., *carbon dioxide* and methane) in the atmosphere. It increases as the percentage of these gases increases.

Heat of evaporation The quantity of energy required to evaporate 1 gram of a substance at a constant temperature.

Heat of fusion The quantity of energy required to melt 1 gram of a substance at a constant temperature.

Hot spot A thin zone of the Earth's *crust* in which one or more columns of *magma* from the underlying *mantle* have risen and solidified.

Intertidal zone The coastal area that is flooded at high *tide* and exposed at low *tide*.

Ion An *atom* or group of atoms that has lost or acquired one or more *electrons* and gained a negative or a positive electric charge as a result.

Lava Molten rock (*magma*) that emerges on the surface of the Earth's *crust*.

Magma Molten rock making up the Earth's *mantle*. Magma is expelled during volcanic eruptions and forms new *crust* along the *mid-ocean ridges*.

Magnetic field, The Earth's A phenomenon caused by the movement of the abundant iron in the fluid part of the Earth's *core*. This movement makes the planet behave like a giant magnet, with a north pole and a south pole. The north-south magnetic axis is declined by about 15° from the Earth's geographical axis.

Mantle The part of the inner Earth between the *crust* and the *core*. The mantle is an enormous mass of very hot rocks in their fluid state. It is around 3,000 kilometers (1,864 mi) thick.

Mid-ocean ridge An immensely long submarine range of mountains found in the middle of the major oceans. The mid-ocean ridges correspond to the gap in the Earth's *crust* between two adjacent *continental plates*. The deep-lying *magma* of the *asthenosphere* slowly rises up to the surface through this gap. It emerges in the form of *lava* and solidifies to form a ridge of basaltic rock creased by deep transverse fractures.

Mud An aggregate composed of *sediments* of *mud* or *clay* or a combination of the two.

Nitrate A plant nutrient of great importance because of the *nitrogen* it contains.

Nitrogen A gaseous chemical element that makes up around four-fifths of the Earth's atmosphere by volume. Nitrogen is an indispensable nutrient for plants and is absorbed by them after having been fixed by certain bacteria in the form of *nitrate*.

Nucleic acids Chemical compounds containing the basis of information relating to the synthesis of *proteins* and therefore the basis of all forms of life.

Nucleotides Basic molecules making up *nucleic acids*. They are composed of a sugar molecule, a phosphate group, and an organic base.

Paleomagnetism The orientation of the magnetism of a rock at the moment in which it solidifies. Paleomagnetism is one of the most reliable means of dating and comparing ancient magmatic rocks.

Pangaea The name given to the supercontinent that existed in the Triassic Period formed from all the *continental plates* while joined together.

pH The changed-sign logarithm of the concentration of hydrogen *ions* in a solution. In practice, a scale from 0 to 14 is used to express the acidity of a solution. Values below 7 indicate acidity, 7 is neutral, and values above 7 indicate alkalinity.

Phosphorus A fairly rare chemical element in the form of phosphates that represent important plant nutrients. It is used by all living things as a basic component of *nucleic acids* and ATP (adenosinetriphosphate, the molecule universally used to accumulate energy).

Polarization The asymmetrical distribution of the *electrons* in a molecule, with the accumulation of a fraction of the negative charge on an *atom* capable of attracting them, and the positive charge on a different *atom*. Water is an example of a polarized molecule.

Proteins Proteins are composed of a specific sequence of hundreds of *amino acids*, of 20 different kinds, linked together and folded to form a secondary and a tertiary structure. Proteins are the principal material that make up living things.

Salinity The amount of *salt* found within something. Sea water has an average salinity of 34.7 parts *salt* to 1,000 parts water.

Salt A chemical compound obtained by the elimination of water during the operation of neutralizing an acid with a corresponding quantity of an alkaline substance. For example, table *salt* (sodium chloride [$NaCl$]) can be obtained by neutralizing hydrochloric acid (HCL) with caustic soda ($NaOH$).

Sand A silicic *sediment* composed of particles with diameters between 6.25 and 20 centimeters (2.46 and 7.87 in).

Sediment Material deriving from the fragmentation and erosion of rocks and the shells and skeletons of organisms, which are then deposited on the ocean floor or on dry land by water, wind, or glaciers.

Silicon A gray, brittle, nonmetallic element (Si). Its oxidized compounds (silicates) constitute the basis of many of the rocks in the Earth's *crust*.

Silt A silicic *sediment* with particles smaller than 0.0625 of a millimeter.

Subduction A progressive process in which one *continental plate* sinks beneath an adjacent plate as the two collide. *Deep-sea trenches* are found along the lines of subduction, where there also are frequent earthquakes.

Surface tension The tendency for liquids to occupy a minimum surface due to the internal forces of molecular cohesion. The surface of a liquid (water, for example) tends to curve and offer sufficient resistance to support small and highly specialized organisms.

Tectonics The science of studying the movement and consequent morphological changes of the Earth's *crust*.

Tides The periodic raising and lowering of the level of the sea. Tides are mainly caused by the gravitational pull of the moon and, to a lesser extent, of the sun.

Thermal capacity The quantity of energy that must be absorbed by a gram of a solid, liquid, or gaseous substance in order to raise its temperature by one degree.

Trade winds Constant winds that blow diagonally from east to west, from the tropics toward the equator, in both hemispheres.

Trade winds originate in a high-pressure band caused by a buildup of warm tropical air between 20 and 30° latitude in both hemispheres.

Tsunami A gigantic *wave* provoked by submarine earthquakes.

Upwellings Vertical currents of cold water rich in nutrient mineral *salts* that rise to the ocean surface. They usually are found all along the *continental margins* where the large oceanic gyres drag the warmer coastal waters out to sea. The warm water is replaced by the colder deep-sea water, and the new supply of nutrients provided leads to a flourishing growth of phytoplankton. The Peru or Humboldt current is a typical upwelling.

Viscosity The internal friction that tends to oppose the flowing of a liquid.

Wave A periodic disturbance in a solid, liquid, or gas caused by energy transmitted through the matter. Waves occur on the surface of the oceans and are generally caused by the wind. A wave is characterized by a high point (called the crest), a low point (called the trough), a wavelength (the distance between two crests), and a wave height (the vertical distance between the tip of the crest and the bottom of the trough).

FURTHER READING

Baines, John D. *Protecting the Oceans*. (Conserving Our World Series). Raintree Steck-Vaughn, 1990

Boyer, Robert E. *Oceanography* (2nd edition). Hubbard Science, 1987

Bramwell, Martyn. *The Oceans* (revised edition). Watts, 1994

Brooks, Felicity. *Seas and Oceans*. (Understanding Geography Series). EDC Publishing, 1987

Conway, Lorraine. *Oceanography*. Good Apple, 1982

Editors, Raintree Steck-Vaughn. *The Raintree Steck-Vaughn Illustrated Science Encyclopedia* (1997 edition). (24 volumes). Raintree Steck-Vaughn, 1997

Fine, John C. *Oceans in Peril*. 1987, Simon and Schuster

Fodor, R. V. *The Strange World of Deep-Sea Vents*. (Earth Processes Series). Enslow Publishers, 1991

Lambert, David. *The Pacific Ocean*. (Seas and Oceans Series). Raintree Steck-Vaughn, 1996

Lambert, David and McConnell, Anita. *Seas and Oceans*. (World of Science Series). Facts on File, 1985

MacRae-Campbell, Linda, et al. *The Ocean Crisis*. (Our Only Earth Series). Zephyr Press, 1990

Markle, Sandra. *Pioneering Ocean Depths*. Simon and Schuster, 1994

Mattson, Robert A. *The Living Ocean*. (Living World Series). Enslow Publishers, 1991

Morgan, Nina. *The Caribbean and the Gulf of Mexico*. (Seas and Oceans Series). Raintree Steck-Vaughn, 1996

————. *The North Sea and the Baltic Sea*. (Seas and Oceans Series). Raintree Steck-Vaughn, 1996

Naden, Corinne J. and Blue, Rose. *The Black Sea*. (Wonders of the World Series). Raintree Steck-Vaughn, 1995

Neal, Philip. *The Oceans*. (Conservation 2000 Series). Trafalgar, 1993

Pifer, Joanne. *EarthWise: Earth's Oceans*. (EarthWise Series). WP Press, 1992

Tesar, Jenny. *Threatened Oceans*. (Our Fragile Planet Series). Facts on File, 1992

Waterlow, Julia. *The Atlantic Ocean*. (Seas and Oceans Series). Raintree Steck-Vaughn, 1996

PICTURE CREDITS

INDEX